D1383255

INVESTIGATING EARTH

Soil

Kate Walker

 **Marshall Cavendish**
Benchmark
New York

Website: www.marshallcavendish.us

This publication represents the opinions and views of the author based on Kate Walker's personal experience, knowledge, and research. The information in this book serves as a general guide only. The author and publisher have used their best efforts in preparing this book and disclaim liability rising directly and indirectly from the use and application of this book.

Other Marshall Cavendish Offices: Marshall Cavendish International (Asia) Private Limited, 1 New Industrial Road, Singapore 536196 • Marshall Cavendish International (Thailand) Co Ltd. 253 Asoke, 12th Flr, Sukhumvit 21 Road, Klongtoey Nua, Wattana, Bangkok 10110, Thailand • Marshall Cavendish (Malaysia) Sdn Bhd, Times Subang, Lot 46, Subang Hi-Tech Industrial Park, Batu Tiga, 40000 Shah Alam, Selangor Darul Ehsan, Malaysia

Marshall Cavendish is a trademark of Times Publishing Limited

All websites were available and accurate when this book was sent to press.

Library of Congress Cataloging-in-Publication Data

Walker, Kate.
    Soil / Kate Walker.
        p. cm. — (Investigating Earth)
    Includes index.
    Summary: "Describes what soil is and why it's important"—Provided by publisher.
    ISBN 978-1-60870-561-0
    1. Soils—Juvenile literature. 2. Soil ecology—Juvenile literature. I. Title.
    S591.3.W33 2012
    631.4—dc22

                                                2010044226

First published in 2011 by
MACMILLAN EDUCATION AUSTRALIA PTY LTD
15–19 Claremont Street, South Yarra 3141

Visit our website at www.macmillan.com.au or go directly to www.macmillanlibrary.com.au

Associated companies and representatives throughout the world.

Copyright text © Kate Walker 2011

Publisher: Carmel Heron   Designer: Kerri Wilson
Commissioning Editor: Niki Horin   Page layout: Romy Pearse
Managing Editor: Vanessa Lanaway   Photo researcher: Legend Images
Editor: Helena Newton   Illustrator: Andrew Hopgood
Proofreader: Kylie Cockle   Production Controller: Vanessa Johnson

Printed in China

Acknowledgments
The author and publisher are grateful to the following for permission to reproduce copyright material:

Front cover photograph: Girl with muddy hands © Corbis/Adie Bush/cultura.

Photographs courtesy of: Corbis/Adie Bush/cultura, 1; Dreamstime.com/Aeolos, 10 (bottom), /Chiyacat, 4 (center right), 18 (right above), /Griffin024, 23, /Klotz, 4 (bottom left), 18 (right below), /Km2008, 4 (center left), 18 (bottom), /Okea, 22, /Rozaliya, 4 (bottom right), 18 (left above), /Rvs, 19 (right), /Slavapolo, 12, /Socrates, 6, 19 (bottom), /Tommason, 19 (left); Getty Images/Peter Anderson, 13, /Jim Brandenburg, 27, Sandy Jones, 5, /Gary John Norman, 14, /Cyril Ruoso/JH Editorial, 26; iStockphoto/Anders Aagesen, 24, /DNY59, 10 (top), /ian francis, 8, /Victor Makhankov, 15, /Andrew Parfenov, 20, /Yarinca, 4 (top); Photolibrary/Peter Bennett, 29, /Gisela Delpho, 28, Photolibrary/ Christian Kapteyn, 30, /Louise Murray/SPL, 25; Pixmac/Tono Balaguer, 10 (center); Shutterstock/Barbro Bergfeldt, 3, 19 (top), /Ali Ender Birer, 18 (center), /Judex, 21, /Susan McKenzie, 4 (bottom center), 18 (left below), /Galushko Sergey, 4 (center), 18 (top).

While every care has been taken to trace and acknowledge copyright, the publisher tenders their apologies for any accidental infringement where copyright has proved untraceable. They would be pleased to come to a suitable arrangement with the rightful owner in each case.

Contents

When a word is printed in **bold**, you can look up its meaning in the Glossary on page 31.

Investigating Earth

We investigate Earth to find out what makes it work.
Earth is made from natural features. Some of these
natural features are living and some are nonliving things.

By investigating Earth we can
learn about how it works.

| Soil | Air | Plants |
| Rocks | Water | Weather |

Soil

Soil is a natural feature of Earth. Soil covers much of Earth's dry land surfaces. Soil also covers the beds of oceans, lakes, and slow-flowing rivers.

A thin bed of soil covers most of Earth's surface.

What Is Soil?

Soil is a nonliving thing. It is loose material on the ground. Plants grow out of soil. Sometimes soil is very thin and sometimes it is many feet deep.

Many giant forest trees grow out of soil that is less than 3 feet (1 meter) deep.

Soil forms in layers, which sit above a layer called **bedrock**. Some soil has just one layer called **topsoil**. Most soil has three layers. Each layer holds a special material.

The three layers of soil sit above bedrock.

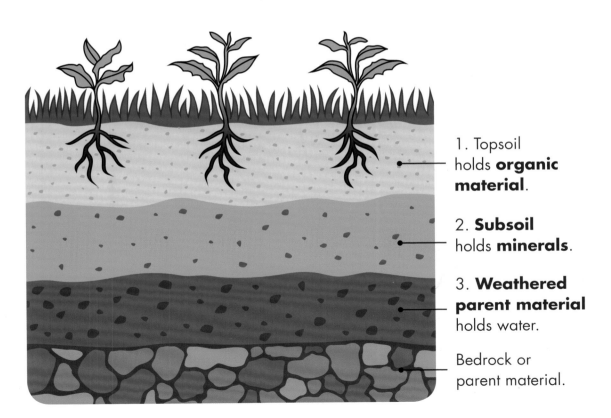

1. Topsoil holds **organic material**.

2. **Subsoil** holds **minerals**.

3. **Weathered parent material** holds water.

Bedrock or parent material.

What Is Soil Made Of?

Soil is made when grains of rock mix with air, water, minerals, and organic material. Organic material found in soil comes from plants and animals that were once alive.

Organic material breaks down in soil and makes the soil dark and crumbly.

Soil also contains living creatures. Soil is home to small animals, such as earthworms, ants, and millipedes. The water in soil also contains billions of tiny, living creatures called **microorganisms**.

Healthy soil contains many living creatures.

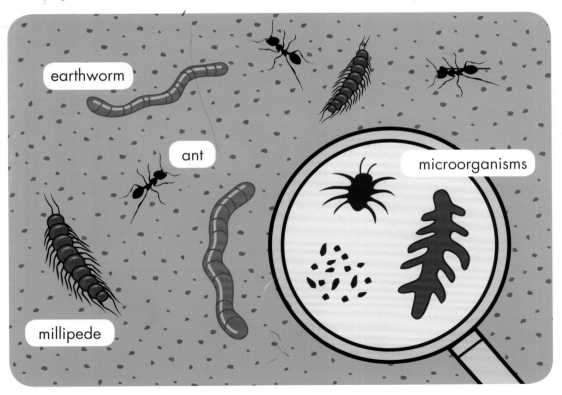

earthworm

ant

microorganisms

millipede

Different Types of Soil

There are three main types of soil. They are found in most places on Earth.

The three main types of soil

1. Sandy soil

2. Clay soil

3. Loam

These three different types of soil are made from different-sized grains.

large grains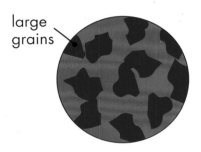

1. Sandy soil has large, rough grains with large spaces between them.

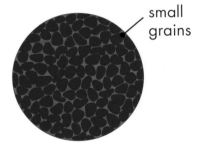 small grains

large grains 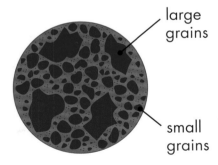 small grains

2. Clay soil has small, smooth grains with small spaces between them.

3. Loam has large and small grains with large and small spaces between them.

Sandy Soil

Sandy soil is dry. Water runs easily through the large spaces between the grains. It carries away valuable minerals that plants need to grow. Sandy soil does not contain much organic material.

Most plants do not grow in sandy soil because the soil lacks water and minerals.

Clay Soil

Clay soil is wet. It traps a lot of water in the small spaces between the grains. Clay soil forms sticky lumps and does not contain much organic material.

A plant's roots stick together in a clump in clay soil.

Loam

Loam is moist. It holds some water in the spaces between the grains. Loam is also soft and crumbly. It holds a lot of organic material and minerals.

Many plants grow well in moist loam.

Loam contains the most soil animals and microorganisms. This is because loam has plenty of air for soil animals to breathe. It also holds water for microorganisms to live in.

Earthworms burrow easily through crumbly loam.

Earth's Soil Cycle

Different materials get mixed together over and over in Earth's soil cycle. These include grains of rock, air, water, minerals, and organic material.

1. Plants and animals are made of organic material. When they die, they fall onto the soil and **decompose**.

4. Plants take nutrients and water from the soil. Plants grow strong and healthy. Some plants are eaten by animals.

Plants, soil animals, and microorganisms are also part of Earth's soil cycle.

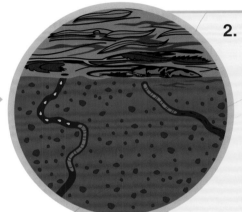

2. Soil animals eat organic material, break it up, and turn it into nutrients. Soil animals also burrow around, spreading organic material, **nutrients**, and air through the soil. Water flows along earthworm tunnels, spreading microorganisms.

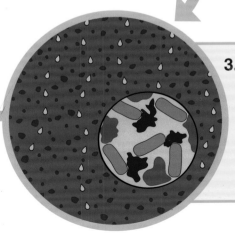

3. Microorganisms eat organic material and **solid** soil minerals. This turns them into nutrients that **dissolve** in water. Water containing dissolved nutrients spreads through the soil.

Why Is Soil Important?

Soil covers most of Earth's land and seafloor surfaces. Soil works together with some of Earth's other natural features. This helps to keep Earth healthy.

Earth has six main natural features that work together to keep Earth healthy.

Air

Plants

Weather

Rocks

Water

Earth

Soil

Soil works together with plants. It also cleans up waste material and helps animals survive.

Soil

Plants
Soil helps plants grow and make new plants.

Waste material
Soil gets rid of Earth's plant and animal waste.

Animals
Soil helps animals survive.

Soil Helps Plants Grow

Soil holds water that plants need to grow. Rain seeps into soil and is stored there. Even in dry weather, plants get water that is stored in moist soil.

Plants grow by taking water from the soil through their roots.

plant

soil

roots

Soil animals and microorganisms also help plants grow. Soil contains solid minerals that plants cannot use. Soil animals and microorganisms turn these into dissolved nutrients that plants can use.

Plants grow strong and healthy in soil that contains lots of soil animals.

Soil Holds Roots and Seeds

Soil gives plants a place to sink their roots and stand upright. Plants need to stand up to spread their leaves to the sun. Plants use sunlight to make food.

Soil helps plants stand up and take in sunlight.

Soil gives plants a place to sow their seeds. Plants drop seeds into the soil. Soil holds warmth from the sun and water that seeds need to help them start growing.

Soil holds warmth and water that helps seeds grow into new plants.

Soil Cleans Up Natural Waste

When plants and animals die, they fall onto Earth and become waste material. Large numbers of plants die every day. Microorganisms and soil animals keep Earth clean by eating plant waste.

A fallen tree is plant waste that can be eaten by microorganisms and soil animals.

Animals die in nature every day. Dead animals can spread diseases that harm other animals and humans. Microorganisms and soil animals eat the bodies of dead animals.

Soil animals and microorganisms prevent diseases by eating dead animals.

Soil Helps Animals Survive

Burrowing animals, such as rabbits, moles, and gophers, use soil for shelter. They make their homes underground by digging tunnels through the soil.

Digging tunnels through the soil protect rabbits from heat, cold, and larger animals.

Some animals use soil to protect their skin. Elephants, buffalo, and pigs cover themselves with dry soil or wet mud. The soil or mud protects them from insect bites and sunburn.

Elephants cover themselves with soil to prevent sunburn and to get rid of insects.

Protecting Soil

Soil is important and needs to be protected. Soil makes plants grow. Plants provide food for humans and animals. Too much **chemical fertilizer** damages soil by killing soil animals and microorganisms.

Humans are damaging soil by using too much chemical fertilizer to grow food.

We can protect the soil by using **organic fertilizers**. Organic fertilizers are made from natural plant and animal waste.

Soil is protected when people grow food using organic fertilizer.

Amazing Soil

Termites are insects that eat plant material, including wood and grasses. They make nests from soil or wood. Some termites build large, spectacular nests from soil, called termite mounds.

Termite mounds are made of soil and are filled with tiny tunnels.

termite mound

Glossary

bedrock — Solid rock below the soil, also known as parent material.

chemical fertilizer — Plant food made by humans and not found in nature.

decompose — Break down naturally.

dissolve — Become part of a liquid, such as water.

microorganisms — Tiny living creatures.

minerals — Hard, nonliving substances found in nature.

organic fertilizers — Natural plant food made from plant and animal waste.

organic material — Matter from living things, such as plants and animals.

nutrients — Substances in soil that plants use to make food.

solid — Keeping the same shape.

subsoil — Soil layer underneath the surface layer or topsoil.

topsoil — Thin surface layer of soil.

weathered parent material — Soil layer containing pieces of broken rock that are the same as the unbroken bedrock, or parent material, below.

Index